A Devotional Prayer Journal

THE SPIRITUAL GROWTH COMPANION
GUIDE **TO THE FIGHT FOR MY LIFE**

50 DAYS

TO

TRIUMPH

TRICIA WYNN PAYNE

DEDICATION

To my beautiful and devoted mother, Joan E. Wynn—
you will triumph through.

ACKNOWLEDGMENTS

The writing of this book or any of my accomplishments would not be possible without God and my community—the tribe of family, friends, and mentors that surround me and uphold me. Thank you, Joan T. Randall and Victorious You Press, for helping this dream become a reality. Thank you, Deirdre Middleton, for your attentive eye and willing spirit. To my father, Courtney Wynn, thank you for always supporting my endeavors.

The writing of this book would not be possible without the undying support and love of my husband, Shawn Payne. Babe, thank you for rowing us through!

TABLE OF CONTENTS

INTRODUCTION

On a sunny spring afternoon, I sat at my kitchen table when the vision for this book swept over me. While I stared at the smoky steam rising in gentle waves from my hot cup of lemon ginger tea, I had an epiphany.

Days earlier, I had submitted the final manuscript for my first book, *The Fight For My Life*, and yet the urge for more awakened within me. "We need more Lord!" I said, as my dear puppy, Dutchess, sat as an attentive audience. "People need more!" I remembered having so much more to share in my first book, but instead, I had determined to save it in my proverbial 'writing parking lot' for another time.

The Fight For My Life chronicles the story of my brush with death, and just how I triumphed through that tragedy. Along the way to healing, I discovered seven precious truths—life lessons I later realized applied to anyone facing a sudden storm, trial, or test of faith. The reviews were overwhelmingly positive. There were constant refrains of, "When is the next book coming?" and "Is there a guide that goes with this?"

This devotional prayer journal, *50 Days to Triumph*, serves as a spiritual growth companion guide to *The Fight For My Life*. It takes you on a 50-day journey through each of the precious discoveries uncovered—remember what God has done; believe what's true; persevere in prayer; guard your mind; stay with people of faith; know God's name, and Jesus has the final say—as shared in my first book. It focuses on one lesson each

1

week for seven weeks. In this journal, you will meditate daily on Scripture, gain encouragement, and challenge yourself with devotional thoughts. It will also prompt you to write for your own self-awareness and end each day with God in prayer. This journal's purpose is to feed your spirit, strengthen your heart, and guide you toward personal growth even while in your storm.

I encourage you to take your time as you journey through each day and approach each page with a prayerful heart—open to hearing from God. He wants to see you through this—whatever challenge you are currently facing. He can help you triumph through your difficulties and even your tragedies. As you take this 50-day journey, my prayer is that you will emerge triumphantly.

Before You Begin...

Before you begin this journey, take a moment to acknowledge your current circumstances and identify your present wishes.

Acknowledge

What adversities, challenges, tragedies, or difficulties are you presently facing?

Assess

What are your thoughts and beliefs about this event or these events?

Admit

How are you feeling about this situation or these situations? What other impact has the circumstance(s) had on yourself and others?

Desire

What would you like to experience in your life by the end of these 50 days?

Pray

Dear Lord, please see what I have written above. As I begin this 50-day journey, I ask that You soften my heart, open my mind, and prepare my entire being so that You will lead me to triumph through this. May Your will be done. In Jesus' name, I pray. Amen.

Week 1
Remember That?

Remember What God Has Done

(Reference Discovery 1 in The Fight For My Life)

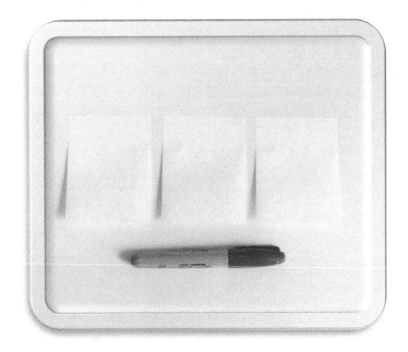

Remember the things I have done in the past. For I alone am God! I am God, and there is none like me.

Isaiah 46:9 NLT

DAY 1

In the beginning God created the heavens and the earth.

Genesis 1:1 NKJV

Before there was you, there was God.

Before your problem(s) emerged, and before this earth formed, there was God. The God, who created this universe, still holds it in His hands. Just look up. See that the moon, sun, and planets all continue in their orbits without you. God performs that. If God accomplishes all of that and continues to sustain all of it, won't He take care of you as well? Remember, God has the solution to every problem that we face. You are in His hands.

Journal Starter:

How does considering all that God accomplished in creating the universe impact my courage to pray today?

Pray

Dear Lord, since You are so mindful of the stars, the sea, the trees, and the grass, and so careful to even give birds a singing voice, surely You are mindful of me. Please help me today, Lord. In Jesus' name, I pray. Amen.

DAY 2

To Him who by wisdom made the heavens, For His mercy endures forever; To Him who laid out the earth above the waters, For His mercy endures forever; To Him who made great lights, For His mercy endures forever— The sun to rule by day, For His mercy endures forever; The moon and stars to rule by night, For His mercy endures forever.

Psalm 136:5–9 NKJV

Look up!

Take a moment to direct your attention away from yourself and look out of your window. Look up. Look around. What do you see? Is the sun still shining even when it hides behind the clouds or lets the moon's glow take center stage? There is an unseen hand that accomplishes this, and His unfailing love is endless. If you look, even through the gloom, there is evidence of God's sustaining presence, for His love never fails.

Journal Starter:

When I look outside today, what evidence do I see of God's sustaining presence?

Pray

Dear Lord, thank You for creating this universe—with its ability to sustain life—with Your wisdom. Today, please open my eyes to see Your past works so that my faith will be strong today. In Jesus' name, I pray. Amen.

DAY 3

The Good Things

Let all that I am praise the Lord; with my whole heart, I will praise his holy name. Let all that I am praise the Lord; may I never forget the good things he does for me.

Psalm 103:1-2 NLT

There's more.

When we are in the midst of our situation, struggle, crisis, or trial, it's easy for problems to be all that we can see, and more so when the stress of it rises to a peak. In these times, our problems mislead us into believing that the adversity we face is all there is or ever was. However, in these moments, we ought to pause and consider the good things. Try it. Go ahead. Think for a moment about just one good thing God has done for you. Recall how it all unfolded. Remember that? Now, as you face your present challenge, think about the good things of the past. They will strengthen you to continue fighting through this day.

Journal Starter:

What good things have I have already experienced?

Pray

Dear Lord, I want to see what is still good even through the unpleasant. Please open my eyes, and help me remember the good things You have already done for me. In Jesus' name, I pray. Amen.

DAY 4

Jesus Was Tempted Too

For we do not have a High Priest who cannot sympathize with our weaknesses, but was in all points tempted as we are, yet without sin.

Hebrews 4:15 NKJV

Jesus understands what you are going through.

Of all the people in your life, Jesus is the one who can truly sympathize with you. He was tempted in the exact way you have been lately. Yes, you read correctly—Jesus experienced temptation. Why? So that He could help you at this very moment, today, and through each day to overcome and to not give in to whatever darkness persistently pulls so strongly at you. Hold on to your faith in Christ through this. He will help you.

Journal Starter:

In my current circumstance, how am I tempted to feel? Why?

Pray

Dear Lord, today I come to You amid my struggle. I ask You to please help me overcome this. I ask you to please help me believe that You will see me through this triumphantly. In Jesus' name, I pray. Amen.

DAY 5

Boundaries and Limitations

Who kept the sea inside its boundaries as it burst from the womb, and as I clothed it with clouds and wrapped it in thick darkness? For I locked it behind barred gates, limiting its shores. I said, 'This far and no farther will you come. Here your proud waves must stop!'

Job 38:8-11 NLT

This will only go so far.

Do you think God is going to allow your adverse circumstance to destroy you? If He can keep the oceans in line, the rivers flowing in their designated path, and the lakes bound in place, surely He can keep your challenge in check too. He draws a boundary line not only for the waters but also for your problems. Even as you consider your challenge, know that it could be much worse, but God has put limits on it.

Journal Starter:

Upon which challenges do I need to perceive God's merciful limitations?

Pray

Dear Lord, thank You for allowing what I am currently facing to be no more than I can handle with You. Help me, Lord, to believe. In Jesus' name, I pray. Amen.

DAY 6

They begged him to let the sick touch at least the fringe of his robe, and all who touched him were healed.

Matthew 14:36 NLT

Jesus remains stocked and ready.

Have you ever gone shopping for an urgently needed item only to find that it is not in stock? Are you even more concerned when it is an essential item? Have you thought to yourself, "What do I do now?"

Jesus never ran out of power, compassion, or time to provide faith-filled seekers with what they desperately required. And the good news is, Jesus has not changed. His doors are always open, and His shelves remain stocked to provide for us in our times of need. He is always available and willing to help.

Journal Starter:

Imagine: You are among those who pursue Jesus. You and the crowd wish desperately to touch the edge of His clothes to receive the healing you all desire. For what need would you now reach out to touch Jesus?

Pray

Dear Lord, as I consider how You aided all who came to You in faith, I am encouraged to ask You to extend that same grace to me this day. Please answer according to Your best desire for me. Lord, I believe in you. Please, take away any disbelief. In Jesus' name, I pray. Amen.

DAY 7

He Loves You

For God so loved the world that He gave His only begotten Son, that whoever believes in Him should not perish but have everlasting life.

John 3:16 NKJV

God loves you.

Even before you knew that God existed, He loved you. Before you acknowledged Him as your God, He gave all of His heart to you. Before you desired His help, He helped you. God wants you to enjoy life. Our Heavenly Father offers everything to you. Before you were born, Jesus planned to save you and to pursue you with His boundless love so that you could thrive. If God can perform all of that, then why wouldn't He help you now?

Journal Starter:

How does accepting God's unconditional love for me impact the way I see my present circumstance?

Pray

Dear Lord, if You loved me so much so that you sacrificed Your only begotten Son to save me, then I trust that You will not withhold what is best for me in this situation. I surrender to You this day's challenge and all my feelings about it. Please help me, Lord. Thank You for what You have already done! In Jesus' name, I pray. Amen

Week 2
Believe What's True

Remember What God Said

(Reference Discovery 2 in The Fight For My Life)

The outer conditions of a person's life will always be found to reflect their inner beliefs.

James Allen

DAY 8

Within Normal Limits

No temptation has overtaken you except such as is common to man; but God is faithful, who will not allow you to be tempted beyond what you are able, but with the temptation will also make the way of escape, that you may be able to bear it.

1 Corinthians 10:13 NKJV

It is not too much.

You are not the only one. You are not alone. Others have had to face what you are currently experiencing. Not only that, but before you received it, He weighed your challenge to ensure that it would be no more than you could handle. God has also promised that He would provide you with an escape route from this temptation, so that it will not overcome you. You are not powerless, nor are you destined for inevitable defeat. With God's help, you will endure, and you will triumph through this.

Journal Starter:

What am I telling myself about my current challenges? Are these thoughts conducive to helping me overcome my challenges?

Pray

Dear Lord, thank You for reminding me that You love me enough to ensure that my present adversity will not be too much for me. Father in Heaven, please show me Your escape route out of this difficulty so that the stress of it will not break me. Help me, Lord, to see Your way through this. In Jesus' name, I pray. Amen.

DAY 9

This Will Build You

My brethren, count it all joy when you fall into various trials, knowing that the testing of your faith produces patience. But let patience have its perfect work, that you may be perfect and complete, lacking nothing.

James 1:2-4 NKJV

Your trial is not meant to break you but to build you.

God sees something of value in you that is more precious than gold. And like gold, you must endure refining to be at your best. Who is to say that the difficulty you face does not serve as a refining agent to bring out the very best in you so that you will be better than you were before? With God, even that is possible.

Journal Starter:

How can my present challenges open new growth opportunities?

Pray

Dear Lord, thank You for seeing the value in me and for trusting in me to go through this test. I am asking You to work within me so I can be a better version of myself. I need Your help so that this challenge will indeed have a good effect and not break my spirit. In Jesus' name, I pray. Amen.

DAY 10

You Will Know

If any of you lacks wisdom, let him ask of God, who gives to all liberally and without reproach, and it will be given to him.

James 1:5 NKJV

God will show you how to handle this. Trust Him.

Yes! This challenge can build you, but only Godly wisdom will show you just what to do as you are in the midst of it. God provides the answers, the direction, and the guidance that you require to navigate this test. If you ask for His help, He will give it. What if you are just one prayer away from figuring this whole thing out?

Journal Starter:

How do I sense God leading me through my current circumstance?

Pray

Dear Lord, I don't know what to do, but my eyes are upon You. Will You grant me the wisdom I need to navigate my current situation? I believe that You will. Please help my disbelief. In Jesus' name, I pray. Amen.

DAY 11

God Is with You

When you pass through the waters, I will be with you; And through the rivers, they shall not overflow you. When you walk through the fire, you shall not be burned, nor shall the flame scorch you.

Isaiah 43:2 NKJV

Difficulties are guaranteed, but so is saving help.

American fictional superheroes always seem to arrive on the scene just in time to save the day. The only problem is they are only fictional characters. What about here? What about now? Most certainly, in this life, we face adversity. It is simply a part of being human. However, there is still saving help—a real Superhero who stays with us. Your troubles do not mean you are unloved or that you will automatically fail. God, who created you, promises to be right there with you as you are going through this turbulent test—to ensure it will neither overwhelm you nor destroy you. He is your ultimate Superhero.

Journal Starter:

How have I already experienced God's presence with me?

Pray

Dear Lord, please come to my rescue. Thank You for promising not to allow these troubles to overtake or destroy me. Thank You for loving me. In Your name, I pray. Amen.

You Can Endure

But those who wait on the Lord Shall renew their strength; they shall mount up with wings like eagles, they shall run and not be weary, they shall walk and not faint.

Isaiah 40:31 NKJV

Check your power source.

Are you running low on the will to fight through this? Who are you expecting and hoping will be there for you? Who are you leaning on to help you? Your doctor? Your friends? Family? Yourself? These power sources are finite—they all have their limitations. But there is one limitless Source. One Source that is infinite in wisdom, strength, and love—that Source is God. You can put all of your proverbial eggs in His basket. You can rest your head on His shoulder. You can expect Him to help you get through this.

Journal Starter:

What is preventing me from leaning on God to help me?

Pray

Dear Lord, I ask You this day to be my power source. Please help me to place all of my hopes and expectations in You. I trust in You. In Jesus' name, I pray. Amen.

DAY 13

You Are Healed

But He was wounded for our transgressions, He was bruised for our iniquities; the chastisement for our peace was upon Him, and by His stripes we are healed.

Isaiah 53:5 NKJV

You are healed.

When you are in the process of healing, you start to heal. God's word cannot lie. Being healed is possible for your mind, body, spirit, and life, but you must believe. As you exercise your faith in Christ, remember what He went through thousands of years ago for you. The cure God offers you in Christ is multifaceted and more helpful than you can even conceive. When you believe and continue your faith in Christ, He grants the type of healing you truly need.

Journal Starter:

In which areas of my life do I desire to realize God's healing?

Pray

Dear Lord, thank You for the way You love me. Thank You for all You have already done. Please mend together the broken pieces of my life. Heal me only in the way You know best. In Jesus' name, I pray. Amen.

DAY 14

You Will Get Through This

For by You I can run against a troop, by my God I can leap over a wall. As for God, His way is perfect; the word of the Lord is proven; He is a shield to all who trust in Him.

Psalm 18:29-30 NKJV

You will get through this.

With God, you will triumph. The life God offers is much more than what is here and now. You will live—if you trust Him. God not only gives you the strength to rise above your problems, but He gives Himself too. By God, you will overcome the challenges and barriers in front of you. They will not defeat you. God fortifies those who trust Him and overthrows the evil that rises against them.

Journal Starter:

Today, how do I desire to experience God?

Pray

Dear Lord, teach me how to let You carry me, deliver me, and fight for me. Please teach me what it means to place all trust in You. In Jesus' name, I pray. Amen.

Week 3

Don't Stop

Persevere in Prayer

(Reference Discovery 6 in The Fight For My Life)

Some people think God does not like to be troubled with our constant coming and asking. The way to trouble God is not to come at all.

D.L. Moody

DAY 15

Self Sufficient?

...if My people who are called by My name will humble themselves, and pray and seek My face, and turn from their wicked ways, then I will hear from heaven, and will forgive their sin and heal their land.

2 Chronicles 7:14 NKJV

Do you need Him?

God desires to make you whole, but you must first acknowledge that you need His help. The first step to getting through this situation and receiving support is to admit that you have a problem. The second step is to confess you cannot tackle this alone and that you need help from Someone greater—from God. You need help from God. We don't have all of the answers to fix our problems. You cannot figure out all the complexities of life by yourself. You will triumph through this when you surrender to God and let Him lead you.

Journal Starter:

Today, what do I admit I need God's help to navigate?

Pray

Dear Lord, I need You. Please save me. I remove my hands from trying to fix this challenge by myself and surrender to You. Help me, Lord. Deliver me, Lord. Please heal all that concerns me this day. In Jesus' name, I pray. Amen.

DAY 16

Time to Turn?

...if My people who are called by My name will humble themselves, and pray and seek My face, and turn from their wicked ways, then I will hear from heaven, and will forgive their sin and heal their land.

2 Chronicles 7:14 NKJV

What if the answer you seek requires you to change a habit?

The old African American saying, "God don't bless mess," is true. As you pray and seek God's face, God might reveal areas in your life that need adjusting. He often shows us where we need a change of course so that our lives are in alignment with His will—from which bountiful blessings can flow. When you look to God for help, He provides the strength you need to make these changes. The good work He initiates in you He will complete. Trust Him.

Journal Starter:

What habit or behavior do I need to change?

Pray

Dear Lord, I surrender myself to You today. Please deliver me from any self-destructive habits. Thank You for promising to finish the good work that You have already started in me. In Jesus' name, I pray. Amen.

DAY 17

He Understands You

Let us therefore come boldly to the throne of grace, that we may obtain mercy and find grace to help in time of need.

Hebrews 4:16 NKJV

Pray boldly.

You can be confident that Jesus not only desires to help you but also understands just how to lead you through this particular trial. How? He experienced the same type of test you are facing today, and He is willing and able to extend to you His abundant kindness wrapped in His saving compassion. Just ask in unwavering faith.

Journal Starter:

In what way(s) am I personally being challenged and tempted?

Pray

Dear Lord, thank You for understanding why I am feeling challenged and tempted today. I give all my feelings about these trials to You. Would you please help me? Please be merciful and gracious to me, O God. In Jesus' name, I pray. Amen.

DAY 18

Anxiety's Antidote

Don't worry about anything; instead, pray about everything. Tell God
what you need, and thank him for all he has done. Then you will
experience God's peace, which exceeds anything we can understand. His
peace will guard your hearts and minds as you live in Christ Jesus.

Philippians 4:6-7 NLT

There is a cure.

Yes, God provides a cure for your anxious mind. However, first, you
must give Him your worries and be thankful for what He has already done.
If your heart, mind, and body are filled with worry and ingratitude, you
will have no room to receive His peace. So, tell Him what's hurting you,
worrying you, and causing you to fear. Let God know all about it and how
it all causes you to think, feel, and act. Then pause and give Him thanks for
what He has already done. He is still the same loving God. He will take care
of you.

Journal Starter:

Today, which anxieties can I surrender? What blessings has God already given to me?

Pray

Dear Lord, thank You for the many blessings You have already given me, and simply for who You are. Please help me to experience life with You and Your peace this day. In Jesus' name, I pray. Amen.

DAY 19

But let him ask in faith, with no doubting, for he who doubts is like a wave of the sea driven and tossed by the wind.

James 1:6 NKJV

Don't know what to do?

Unsure how to navigate your circumstance or even this day? Instead of worrying about it, ask God what to do. God takes no pleasure in your confusion, elevated stress levels, and anxiety. He wants to direct your steps through each day, but you've got to ask Him without doubting Him.

There may be instances where we are unsure whether God will grant our requests exactly as we have asked because our desires can, at times, be damaging. However, you need not wonder if God will give wisdom. He said He would.

Journal Starter:

In which direction do I perceive God leading me today?

Pray

Dear Lord, thank You for being the One I can turn to when I don't know what to do. While I cannot see the way through this, I believe You do. Please show me Your way, Lord. In Jesus' name, I pray. Amen.

DAY 20

As it is in Heaven

Your kingdom come. Your will be done on earth as it is in heaven.

Matthew 6:10 NKJV

Don't know what to ask God for today?

Try praying the Our Father prayer, and end with, "Your will be done on earth as it is in heaven." Any prayer of faith—made in harmony with God's will—shall be heard and answered. So why not ask God for His plans, intentions, purposes, and outcomes to be done today—not only in your life but in the lives of others? God's intentions are good. Asking for His will to be done is not accepting defeat, it's receiving victory.

Journal Starter:

What thoughts and feelings come to mind when I consider God's will for me?

Pray

Dear Lord, I release to You my ideas of what I think I need today and open my hands and heart to receive Your will for me. May Your will be done today as it is in heaven. In Jesus' name, I pray. Amen.

DAY 21

Keep on Praying

Keep on asking, and you will receive what you ask for. Keep on seeking, and you will find. Keep on knocking, and the door will be opened to you. For everyone who asks, receives. Everyone who seeks, finds. And to everyone who knocks, the door will be opened.

Matthew 7:7-8 NLT

Keep on asking. Don't stop.

There are unclaimed blessings with your name on them in heaven that you will receive only by persistently praying in faith. This constant action of intentionally praying is not because God's heart needs to be softened or requires convincing to grant your needs. Persevering in prayer impacts our faith and allows us to receive what God longs to give us. So, keep on praying. Don't stop. You will receive God's best for your life today.

Journal Starter:

What am I going to keep on praying about?

Pray

Dear Lord, once again, I bring before You my petition. Hear me, O Lord, and please answer according to Your will. Prepare me to receive Your very best blessings for me and my life. In Jesus' name, I pray. Amen.

Week 4

Praise More

Guard Your Mind

(Reference Discovery 3 in The Fight For My Life)

It is a positive duty to resist melancholy, discontented thoughts and feelings—as much a duty as it is to pray.

Ellen G. White

DAY 22

Think on These Things

Finally, brethren, whatever things are true, whatever things are noble, whatever things are just, whatever things are pure, whatever things are lovely, whatever things are of good report, if there is any virtue and if there is anything praiseworthy—meditate on these things.

Philippians 4:8 NKJV

Think about the good things.

You can choose to focus on what is going well. Paul admonished the Christians in Philippi for not thinking positively regardless of their situation. The Holy Spirit moved Paul to exhort his readers to meditate on the positive things. Even when locked up, he was committed to telling others of Jesus. He wrote that chapter from jail, after all!

Today, even in the very heart of your trial, you can choose to think about what is still beautiful, pleasant, and going well in your life. Why? Because it will help you triumph through this.

Journal Starter:

What positive things can I choose to meditate on today?

Pray

Dear Lord, please search me and know my heart; try me and know my anxieties. If there is any wicked way in me, kindly lead me in Your everlasting good way. Help me this day to remain focused on the positive things. In Jesus' name, I pray. Amen.

Don't copy the behavior and customs of this world, but let God transform you into a new person by changing the way you think. Then you will learn to know God's will for you, which is good and pleasing and perfect.

Romans 12:2 NLT

Are you having a difficult time focusing on what's right?

Are you finding it challenging to manage your thoughts? Don't fear. God can help you, but you must let Him. That's right. You can choose to allow God to affect your heart and mind.

God desires to elevate your thinking, even if your family history and genetic makeup say otherwise. He can help you. Will you let Him do it?

Journal Starter:

In which areas do I desire God to impact my thinking?

Pray

Dear Lord, may all of my words and all of my thoughts be pleasing to You—for You are my rescuer and my mainstay. In Jesus' name, I pray. Amen.

DAY 24

Be Deliberate

Guard your heart above all else, for it determines the course of your life.

Proverbs 4:23 NLT

A good outcome begins with deliberate thinking.

It can be challenging to remain positive when we are hurting. At times, the pain can overshadow everything—leaving us feeling hopeless. That's why it is so vital to protect our minds against influences that render us depressed and distracted from God's grace—especially as we navigate life storms. Maintaining a spirit of gratitude as you live each day is one way to purposefully protect your mind and keep you on the best course for your life.

Journal Starter:

To better guard my mind, what habits can I implement?

Pray

Dear Lord, when I am tempted to remain in despair, please help me to remember reasons to be thankful and lead me to praise Your holy name. In Jesus' name, I pray. Amen.

DAY 25

Focus

You will keep in perfect peace all who trust in you, all whose thoughts are fixed on you!

Isaiah 26:3 NLT

Need more peace?

Try resting your mind and heart on God's love. When you do, you can't help but rejoice! Don Moen wrote a beautiful song that says,

Think about His love, think about His goodness

Think about His grace that's brought us through

For as high as the heavens above

So great the measure of our Father's love

Great is the measure of our Father's love

When your heart is full of gratitude, there is little room for anxiety.

Journal Starter:

For what am I thankful today?

Pray

Dear Lord, when my heart feels anxious and weary, please focus my attention on Your unfailing love, and open my lips to praise You. In Jesus' name, I pray. Amen.

DAY 26

Like Medicine

A merry heart does good, like medicine, but a broken spirit dries the bones.

Proverbs 17:22 NKJV

It's free!

There are no doctor's orders nor health insurance needed for this cure. A happy, joy-filled heart is as effective as medicine. Our state of mind not only impacts our actions but also impacts our health. Filling our hearts and minds with reasons to be joy-filled gives us life. As you navigate today's challenge, what reason(s) do you have to be grateful and happy? Take a break, throw your head back, and let out a good belly laugh. Your life could depend on it.

Journal Starter:

How can I make time to laugh and have fun today?

Pray

Dear Lord, my heart rejoices in Your goodness toward me. This day, may my mind rest ever on Your kindness and the many blessings You shower into my life. In Jesus' name, I pray. Amen.

DAY 27

It's Up to You

So letting your sinful nature control your mind leads to death. But letting the Spirit control your mind leads to life and peace.

Romans 8:6 NLT

It's your choice.

Allowing God into your heart and permitting Him to lead your mind brings peace and gives life. Today, peace and life can be yours. It's up to you.

While the present challenge may seem like the end, with the Holy Spirit in your heart, even this challenge can work in your favor in the end. So, why not accept God into your heart, even during this test, and experience the peace He promises to give?

Journal Starter:

What is hindering me from fully accepting God into my heart today?

Pray

Dear Lord, please forgive me for my sins. Please come into my heart. Please grant me Your peace and the life You promise to give me. May the Holy Spirit regulate my thoughts. In Jesus' name, I pray. Amen.

DAY 28

More to Come

Think about the things of heaven, not the things of earth.

Colossians 3:2 NLT

Are you feeling overwhelmed? Try thinking ahead.

When writing to people who had newly accepted Christ into their hearts, Paul advised them to set their sights on heaven and the fact that Jesus would return. Why? So that they would not be overwhelmed by their present challenges and slip into temptation.

When it seems like your challenge is crushing you, try pausing and taking the time to think ahead. What will it be like for you when Christ returns?

Journal Starter:

When I consider the reality of heaven, how does it impact my outlook?

Pray

Dear Lord, when I am overwhelmed, help me remember that my trouble will not last always. Please give me the strength to hold on to You through this and not yield to temptation. In Jesus' name, I pray. Amen.

Week 5

Not All by Yourself

Stay with People of Faith

(Reference Discovery 4 in The Fight For My Life)

But woe to him who is alone when he falls, for he has no one to help him up.

Ecclesiastes 4:10 NKJV

71

DAY 29

Companionship... a Necessity

And being let go, they went to their own companions and reported all that the chief priests and elders had said to them.

Acts 4:23 NKJV

Ever wonder if you would be a nuisance if you told others about your difficulties?

Some believe that you cannot trust others to offer their genuine concern and aid in times of crisis. However, we gain great insight from Jesus and his apostles—they shared their burdens. And what was the outcome? They received the strength needed to keep on going—the will to triumph through adversity.

Journal Starter:

How do I feel about sharing my present adversity with others? Why?

Pray

*Dear Lord, thank You for always being the one in whom I find safety.
Please show me the people You have provided to be my necessary
companions during my current challenge. In Jesus' name, I pray. Amen.*

DAY 30

Too Much for Just You

So Moses' father-in-law said to him, "The thing that you do is not good. Both you and these people who are with you will surely wear yourselves out. For this thing is too much for you; you are not able to perform it by yourself.

Exodus 18:17-18 NKJV

Ever feel like this thing is too much for you?

Well, what if this was not meant for only you to bear, figure out, navigate, and fix? God entrusted Moses with an enormous task. Yet, even in that, God did not expect him to carry it out on his own. God guided Moses to people who would help him fulfill his task. There is no shame in admitting that we need others to help us. Asking for help requires vulnerability, but in the long run, it will be worth it.

Journal Starter:

In my present circumstance, who are the people of faith, love, and wisdom I know?

Pray

Dear Lord, thank You for promising to neither leave nor forsake me. Thank You for the gift of friendship and community that You provide me. Thank You for guiding me to the people who are going to support me through my current obstacles and for granting me the courage to ask for help. In Jesus' name, I pray. Amen.

DAY 31

Then Esther told them to reply to Mordecai: "Go, gather all the Jews who are present in Shushan, and fast for me; neither eat nor drink for three days, night or day. My maids and I will fast likewise. And so I will go to the king, which is against the law; and if I perish, I perish!"

Esther 4:15-16 NKJV

Fast and pray.

Unsure what others can do to help you? Try asking them to pray and fast with you and for you. You don't have to go at this alone. When faced with a life or death moment, Queen Esther depended on the Jewish people in the city to fast with her. What if your shift is just a collective prayer away? Finding a few people to fast with you can change the course of not only this circumstance, but of your life.

Journal Starter:

If I were to pray and fast, who could I ask to join me? When would I start and end? What would be my desired outcome?

Pray

Dear Lord, today I receive Your strength and wisdom to ask others to pray and fast for and with me. Please prompt people of faith to join with me, and may I do the same in the lives of others. In Jesus' name, I pray. Amen.

DAY 32

Covered

Then Jonathan and David made a covenant, because he loved him as his own soul. And Jonathan took off the robe that was on him and gave it to David, with his armor, even to his sword and his bow and his belt.

1 Samuel 18:3-4 NKJV

Who has your back?

Having at least one trusted friend can save your life. David's life was spared at least once from the hands of his jealous father-in-law because of his friend Jonathan's advice and help. Johnathan's friendship protected David.

We were not meant to live isolated from others, whether it be in times of prosperity or through times of great difficulty. In our times of trial, friendships can be a source of strength and even lifesaving help.

Journal Starter:

For which friendships am I grateful and why?

Pray

Dear Lord, thank You for Your gift of friendship. Please show me how to better foster friendships, and be a good friend to the people You have placed in my life. In Jesus' name, I pray. Amen.

DAY 33

Choose to Love

But Ruth replied, "Don't ask me to leave you and turn back. Wherever you go, I will go; wherever you live, I will live. Your people will be my people, and your God will be my God. Wherever you die, I will die, and there I will be buried. May the Lord punish me severely if I allow anything but death to separate us!"

Ruth 1:16-17 NLT

Who do you love?

Even at your worst moment, you can choose to love someone and treat them like you wish to be treated. Ruth made that choice. As a recent widow, she pledged a commitment and her lifelong presence to her deceased husband's mother. No strings attached. No evidence of rewards or benefits. No promises for a better future. She chose to love through her tragedy, and, in the end, that choice brought her an abundant life.

Journal Starter:

Who in my life needs my love the most?

Pray

Dear Lord, lead me to show love to someone, even as I go through my trials each day. Thank You for the blessed life and abundant joy this will bring me. In Jesus' name, I pray. Amen.

DAY 34

Surrounded

...they stoned Paul and dragged him out of the city, supposing him to be dead. However, when the disciples gathered around him, he rose up ...

Acts 14:19-20 NKJV

Choose your company wisely—one day, your life may depend on it.

Paul was stoned, dragged, discarded, and pronounced dead. After his execution, Paul's friends surrounded him. What would have happened to Paul if he had no such community? He could have died there—alone. If you want to make room for miracles in your life, surround yourself with God-fearing people of faith and love.

Journal Starter:

Why do I think Paul got up?

Pray

Dear Lord, please keep me in a community of Believers that care about me enough to believe for me, especially when I am too beaten to believe for myself. In Jesus' name, I pray. Amen.

DAY 35

But Moses' hands became heavy; so they took a stone and put it under him, and he sat on it. And Aaron and Hur supported his hands, one on one side, and the other on the other side; and his hands were steady until the going down of the sun.

Exodus 17:12 NKJV

It's okay to accept help.

When people's lives depended on him, Moses realized he could not do his part of praying with upraised hands alone. This faith-filled leader needed help. He required support in leading the people to triumph. Moses believed in God; however, he would have failed to carry out his task without the aid of those closest to him. People would have perished. Thankfully, Moses asked for and received help. The hands of his friends lifted him up and steadied him while he completed his task for God.

Journal Starter:

Who can I depend on today to help steady me?

Pray

Dear Lord, if my hands feel heavy and I feel unable to go on, help me to recognize the people You have sent to support me through this day and this trial. In Jesus' name, I pray. Amen.

Week 6

What Did You Say Your Name Was Again?

Know God's Name

(Reference Discovery 5 in The Fight For My Life)

Faith in God is not merely to believe that He exists, but to truly believe the right thing about His nature and character.

Tricia Wynn Payne

DAY 36

Let Me Introduce Myself

Then the Lord came down in a cloud and stood there with him; and he called out his own name, Yahweh.

Exodus 34:5 NLT

God wants you to know His name.

More than just as an intellectual acknowledgment of His title, He wants you to know who He is by experiencing Him through your difficulties and perplexities. God wants you to know Him. He stood and declared His name centuries ago, and His voice still echoes in us today. The God of creation declares to you that He is Yahweh. God is responsible for keeping the promises He makes. He will do as He says.

Journal Starter:

What do I think about God and His character?

Pray

Dear Lord, please open my heart to know You more. O God, clear my
eyes so that I can see You, even when I'm hurting. In Jesus' name, I pray.
Amen.

DAY 37

I Am Compassion

The Lord passed in front of Moses, calling out, "Yahweh! The Lord! The God of compassion and mercy..."

Exodus 34:6 NLT

God cares.

He can't help Himself. That's just who He is. Some days, you might wonder if He is still "up there," and if He still responds to prayers. He does. God cares about what you are going through. He is deeply interested in you and concerned about your wellbeing. Not only that, but His compassion moves Him to act on your behalf. He takes no delight in your suffering. He knows just how much you can handle. He will get you through this. That's just who He is.

Journal Starter:

Today, how do I need to experience God's compassion?

Pray

Dear Lord, Compassionate God, please have mercy on me. In Jesus' name, Amen.

DAY 38

I Am Gracious

And the Lord passed before him and proclaimed, "The Lord, The Lord God, merciful and gracious..."

Exodus 34:6 NKJV

God gives you good things you don't deserve.

Even amidst your tragedies, He still blesses you with favors you could never earn. That's right! Today, His kindness to you surpasses reasonable human expectations. Yes, even as you cross through valleys, God's favor, His abundant favor, is present, and even more is available to you—if you ask and believe. You can trust God's grace—that's who He is. He cannot help Himself.

Journal Starter:

Because God gives me good things I do not deserve, today, I can

boldly ask?

Pray

Dear Lord, thank You for being so good to me. Your kindness surpasses my greatest expectations. Please allow Your gracious way in my life today. In Jesus' name, I pray. Amen.

DAY 39

And the Lord passed before him, and proclaimed, "The Lord, The Lord God, merciful and gracious, longsuffering..."

Exodus 34:6 NKJV

God bears with us.

He patiently waits through our temper tantrums, missteps, and misguided stubborn will. That's His nature. He neither turns His back on you nor withholds his love and care from you—even when you turn your back on Him. People disappoint us in that way, but God does not. He suffers with us and yearns for us to turn to Him so that we experience rest and abundance in our lives.

Journal Starter:

What growth opportunities have my current difficulties exposed?

Pray

Dear Lord, thank You for suffering long with me. Please forgive me for my missteps and distrust of You. Help me trust You, yield to You, and follow You. In Jesus' name, I pray. Amen.

DAY 40

I Am Loyal

And the Lord passed before him, and proclaimed, "The Lord, The Lord God, merciful and gracious, longsuffering, and abounding in goodness and truth..."

Exodus 34:6 NKJV

God is loyal.

He is right there with you. He will keep His promises to you even when you falter. He will not fail you.

God lavishes His children with overflowing, limitless love. He will always do His part. You can depend on Him to take care of you at all times and in every situation. That's just who He is!

Journal Starter:

What do I believe about God's love for me?

Pray

Dear Lord, thank You for loving me the way You do. Even when I am not faithful, You are faithful! Please help me to truly believe in who You are. In Jesus' name, I pray. Amen.

DAY 41

And the Lord passed before him, and proclaimed, "The Lord, The Lord God, merciful and gracious, longsuffering, and abounding in goodness and truth..."

Exodus 34:6 NKJV

God is the truth.

He is abundantly reliable, so much more so than your automatic clock, GPS, or Smart Wallet. Who He is and what He says is steadfast and unfailing. You can put all of your trust in Him—without the expectation of failure. What peace could be yours today if you choose to believe that He is who He says He is? God's loving security for you will not fail. It cannot fail. That's just who He is!

Journal Starter:

How will believing that God is reliable help me today?

Pray

Dear Lord, show me how to place all of the weight of my expectations in You because I know You cannot fail. I believe You will not fail me. Please help me to trust that You are indeed the truth. In Jesus' name, I pray.
Amen.

DAY 42

And he said, "Please show me Your glory." Then He said, "I will make all My goodness pass before you, and I will proclaim the name of the Lord before you..."

Exodus 33:18-19 NKJV

In our challenges, God's glory shines the brightest.

The glorious presence of God reveals itself amidst your most difficult circumstances. Most often, at the very pinnacle of our tragedies and in the heart of our uncertainties, it is here that we can discern more of the Glory of God. If we seek Him out, we can experience the essence of who He is. He is compassionate, gracious, patient, loyal, and the truth. When trudging through our agony, God's Glory most clearly shows in our suffering.

Journal Starter:

Over the past 40 days, what have you discovered about God?

Pray

Dear Lord, thank You for being with me and allowing me to see Your glory. On days when my vision is dim, You still shine through. Lord, I want to know Your name. In Jesus' name, I pray. Amen.

Week 7

Science Isn't Final

Jesus Has the Final Say

(Reference Discovery 7 in The Fight For My Life)

The Christian never works toward victory, he always works FROM victory.

Henry Blackaby

DAY 43

Believe Greater

"Now unto him that is able to do exceeding abundantly above all that we ask or think, according to the power that worketh in us, Unto him be glory in the church by Christ Jesus throughout all ages, world without end. Amen."

Ephesians 3:20-21 KJV

Believe greater!

God can achieve many things through you. God can accomplish even more than your imagination can daydream. You only need to trust in Him to overcome your tragedies. What if God takes your tragedy and gives it a new purpose? What if He creates a positive result that produces a much greater good? This positive result will leave ripples in your life, and these ripples will positively affect your friends, family, relationships, and the world around you. It will lead to good things.

Trust Him.

Journal Starter:

What good can I see arising as a result of my current circumstances?

Pray

Dear Lord, it can be hard to see anything great coming from this challenge. Help me to believe that You will do great things—more than I can ever imagine. In Jesus' name, I pray. Amen.

You Can Trust Him

I will worship toward Your holy temple, and praise Your name for Your lovingkindness and your truth; for You have magnified Your word above all Your name.

Psalm 138:2 NKJV

Are you wondering if God keeps His promises?

God's name and the reputation of His character are on the line if He should fail you. In other words, regardless of how dire your situation appears, and, even when others say there is no hope, God's word, His intention, and His plan for you will stand. His word will not fail. God's character will not allow it. So even before you see the way out, you can trust Him. His love will never fail you.

Journal Starter:

Because of who he is, God always keeps His promises. He is backed by all the honor that comes with His holy name. How does that fact give me hope today? Why?

Pray

Dear Lord, please help me to trust You over my feelings today. In Jesus' name, I pray. Amen.

DAY 45

Never Abandoned

The Lord will perfect that which concerns me; Your mercy, O Lord, endures forever; do not forsake the works of Your hands.

Psalm 138:8 NKJV

God will not forsake you.

The good work that He has been doing—in you, through your trial—in His hands will accomplish something more for you than the suffering you have known. He will not leave you unfinished. God will bring about His plan for your life, but you have got to trust Him. Even throughout your difficulties, God was working out His good plans for you. He will not abandon you. Trust Him beyond what you can see today.

Journal Starter:

Today, I understand that God will not abandon me nor leave me incomplete. Why does that fact give me confidence?

Pray

Dear Lord, please help me to trust You today, even when I cannot see my way out. Please help me to hope in You, even while my way is not yet clear. In Jesus' name, I pray. Amen.

Follow His Direction

Trust in the Lord with all your heart, and lean not on your own understanding; in all your ways acknowledge Him, and He shall direct your paths.

Proverbs 3:5-6 NKJV

When God directs, we ought to listen.

While things may not be as you would like them to be today, you could still choose to commit your entire being to God and trust Him. He will work out His best plan for you. That's His responsibility.

What should you do? Try leaning on Him. Put the entire weight of your expectations on God. And, in the strength that He gives you, follow His direction.

Journal Starter:

What instructions has God given me that I have yet to follow?

Pray

Dear Lord, please help me to rely on You more than anyone else or anything else in my life. Please strengthen my faith so that I will follow Your guidance in my life. In Jesus' name, I pray. Amen.

DAY 47

And we know that all things work together for good to those who love God, to those who are the called according to His purpose.

Romans 8:28 NKJV

Synergy.

When the combined effect is greater than the separate effects of two or more agents, you have what we call synergy. God can work or synergize all that happens in your life to bring about a positive effect for you and in your world. What you are going through right now, once in God's hands, will yield something greater. Trust Him.

Journal Starter:

Though I may not see it now, why does knowing that God will yield something more for those who love Him assure me?

Pray

Dear Lord, I am grateful that You know just how to bring about something greater even from my challenges. Please help me to live each day loving You. In Jesus' name, I pray. Amen.

DAY 48

Never Incomplete

And I am certain that God, who began the good work within you, will continue his work until it is finally finished on the day when Christ Jesus returns.

Philippians 1:6 NLT

God completes what He starts.

Your test does not mean that He has forsaken you. He continues His great work within you even through your trial. Your challenge, in His hands, works to build you up—not break you down. Yes, you will triumph through this!

You may triumph as a result of this trial. You may achieve or realize in your life something far more valuable than you would have had you not had the adversity. You may successfully overcome your challenge—trampling it under your feet or bulldozing right through it. Alternately the triumph you experience could be one where the adversity remains; however, you and those around you grow from the experience.

He has started a great work within you, and this situation will not derail God's best for you. He will complete what He started.

Journal Starter:

How does knowing that God promises to complete what He began impact my thoughts? What does that lead me to request? What does that cause me to believe about my circumstance?

Pray

Dear Lord, thank You for leading me through these past seven weeks. I hold on to the promise that You will finish the good work You have started within me. This test is not the end. You have the last word. I will always trust You. In Jesus' name, I pray. Amen.

Reflect

DAY 49

What have you experienced in your life these 49 days?

DAY 50

...looking unto Jesus, the author and finisher of our faith, who for the joy that was set before Him endured the cross, despising the shame, and has sat down at the right hand of the throne of God. For consider Him who endured such hostility from sinners against Himself, lest you become weary and discouraged in your souls.

Hebrews 12:2-3 NKJV

Jesus won.

Christ endured great pain to help you triumph through yours. For Jesus, the cross was unavoidable, His pain a necessity, and His death tragic. But Jesus endured, and by it accomplished something far greater—He atoned for our sins, making life after death possible for all who believe (John 3:16). The presence of adversity in your life does not mean God has forsaken you, nor does it mean that you have lost His protection and love. Life is complicated and, at times, very unpleasant, but in God's hands, your pain is not wasted. If you allow Him, Jesus will even take that pain and use it to accomplish His good work in you. When you trust God, you win because He has already won.

Journal Starter:

Look back to the section, "Before You Begin." What growth have you experienced in your life since beginning this 50-day journey?

Acknowledge

What is the status of the adversities, challenges, tragedies, or difficulties you identified on day one?

Assess

How are you currently thinking about the challenges you identified on day one?

Admit

How are you currently feeling about your circumstances? Over the past 50 days, how have your actions impacted your challenges?

In what way does knowing that Jesus also suffered and triumphed through assure you?

Pray

Dear Lord, thank You for the victory I have in You, and for leading me to triumph through. Please help me to keep my gaze on You and my hope in You each day. Use me, Lord, along with the lessons You have taught me, to help someone else as they navigate their adversities. In Jesus' name, I pray. Amen.

BEFORE YOU GO

Here on earth, we will have trials and sorrows; nevertheless, Christ has said we should take heart because He has "overcome the world" (John 16:33 NKJV). You have an advocate in heaven who is cheering for you to triumph through life's difficulties because he has also experienced and triumphed through them. Jesus is qualified and able to lead you and help you.

Yes, triumph may look differently for you than it appears for your neighbor. Triumphing through your challenge does not always mean it will go away. Your cancer may not go into remission. You may lose your house, apartment, or place of safety. You may have to say goodbye to a loved one. Sometimes, our prayers are not answered in the way we expect. However, as you go through your troubles, do not doubt that God is still accomplishing His good purposes in your life.

How can you continue to triumph? Remember what God has done, believe what's true, persevere in prayer, guard your mind, stay with people of faith, know God's name, and understand that Jesus has the final say.

When we trust Him, as we go through the heart of it, we experience triumph. Somehow, in God's hands, our pain is repurposed and brings out something exceptional in us. We may not see it now, but one day, like the Bible writer Paul, we will declare, "For I consider that the sufferings of this present time are not worthy to be compared with the glory which shall be revealed in us" (Romans 8:18 NKJV).

50 DAYS TO TRIUMPH
Daily Scriptures

Week 1

Genesis 1:1

Psalm 136:5-9

Psalm 103:1-2

Hebrews 4:15

Job 38:8-11

Matthew 14:36

John 3:16

Week 2

1 Corinthians 10:13

James 1:2-4

James 1:5

Isaiah 43:2

Isaiah 40:31

Isaiah 53:5

Psalm 18:29-30

Week 3

2 Chronicles 7:14

Hebrews 4:16

Philippians 4:6-7

James 1:6

Matthew 6:10

Matthew 7:7-8

Week 4

Philippians 4:8

Romans 12:2

Proverbs 4:23

Isaiah 26:3

Proverbs 17:22

Romans 8:6

Colossians 3:2

Week 5

Acts 4:23

Exodus 18:17-18

Esther 4:15-16

1 Samuel 18:3-4

Ruth 1:16-17

Acts 14:19-20

Exodus 17:12

Week 6

Exodus 34:5

Exodus 34:6

Exodus 33:18-19

Week 7

Ephesians 3:20-21

Psalm 138:2

Psalm 138:8

Proverbs 3:5-6

Romans 8:28

Philippians 1:6

Day 50

Hebrews 12:2-3

ABOUT THE AUTHOR

Tricia Wynn Payne is a sought-after international Christian speaker and preacher who has enjoyed sharing life-transforming messages of encouragement, empowerment, and hope for over 20 years. Inspired by suffering life-threatening complications after undergoing a minor outpatient procedure, she now seeks to empower individuals to take the limits off and live to their purposed potential through her preaching, writing, coaching, and teaching.

She transitioned from a nine-year career as a physical therapist to serve full-time in pastoral ministry because of her passion for inspiring others with the life-empowering message of God's love. As a pastor, she has initiated innovative youth and young adult focused ministries, developed community partnerships and outreach programs assisting underprivileged, at-risk, and refugee populations.

While conducting young adult outreach in Chicago, Illinois, she met Kansas City, Missouri, native Shawn Payne, who would later become the love of her life and her husband.

CONNECT WITH TRICIA WYNN PAYNE

Email: TriciaWynnPayne@gmail.com

Facebook: facebook.com/TriciaWynnPayne

Instagram: instagram.com/triciawynnpayne

TriciaWynnPayne.com

OTHER WORK BY TRICIA WYNN PAYNE

The Fight For My Life: What I Discovered as I Triumphed Through Tragedy

Made in United States
Orlando, FL
03 December 2021